STRIVING
TOWARD
PERFECTION

Biblical and Practical Approaches to Spiritual Formation

STRIVING TOWARD PERFECTION

Biblical and Practical Approaches to Spiritual Formation

Compiled by Eugene Carvalho

To the Body of Christ.
May this compilation bless you richly!
With love…

TABLE OF CONTENTS

PURPOSE AND ACKNOWLEDGEMENTS

The infallible Word of God for faith and conduct informs us that the Holy Spirit gives gifts to men and women of the Body of Christ. It states: "the gifts edify the body for the building up of the saints" (Eph. 4:12). I hope the talents and gifts the Lord has given me will be a blessing to someone else through the reading of this compilation.

I am grateful for the love from all family members, especially my wonderful wife Mercedes Carvalho. I am also grateful for the knowledge, wisdom and love of many pastors, teachers, and saints that the Lord has used to bless me. Lastly, I must not forget a special thank you to Kathryn Regan for proofreading this material.

SPIRITUAL DISIPLINES

Faith and spiritual disciplines assist Christians to have abundance in every area of life and ministry. Faith and spiritual disciplines are avenues in which a born-again believer can grow and allow spiritual formation to manifest. They make up who we are and who we will become: our Christian character. It takes faith, daily devotion and consistency to submit to the Holy Spirit and let Him have His way in every area of our life. It takes stern day-to-day diligence. The Bible says, "The thief cometh not, but for to steal, and to kill, and to destroy: I am come that they might have life, and that they might have it more abundantly" (Jn. 10:10 KJV). God wants you to prosper in every area.

This is why I will be starting this compilation discussing different types of spiritual disciplines which are avenues the Lord uses to enrich our Heavenly calling. The Bible says, "Beloved, I wish above all things that thou mayest prosper and be in health, even as thy soul prospereth" (3 Jn. 1:2 KJV).

Moving forward and maturing by allowing the Holy Spirit to continually change us is central to our walk with Christ. I read not long ago from an unknown author that: "Until the pain of staying the same is greater than the pain of change, some people will never change." Because of our love for Christ, we must move forward in Him no matter what the cost may be. The debt of love is measured by the amount of the sacrifice.

There are so many books that have helped me tremendously regarding my daily spiritual disciplines. However, I do have a favorite titled: *Celebration of Discipline* by Richard Foster. In the contents of his book, he breaks down spiritual disciplines in the following manner. I had planned to mention most of them so I feel I should offer them in the order in which the author discussed them. It may help individuals to understand them better.

Inward Disciplines:
Meditation, Prayer, Fasting, Study

Outward Disciplines:
Simplicity, Solitude, Submission, Service

Corporate Disciplines:
Confession, Worship, Guidance, Celebration

Discipline #1 – Meditation on God's Word

I have chosen this discipline first also because of what I am informed in Scripture: "Finally, be strong in the Lord and in His mighty power. Put on the full armor of God so that you can take your stand against the devil's schemes. For our struggle is not against flesh and blood, but against the rulers, against the authorities, against the powers of this dark world and against the spiritual forces of evil in the heavenly realms. Therefore put on the full armor of God, so that when the day of evil comes, you may be able to stand your ground, and after you have done everything, to stand. Stand firm then, with the belt of truth buckled around your waist, with the breastplate of righteousness in place, and with your feet fitted with the readiness that comes from the gospel of peace" (Eph. 6:10-15).

Right there! Did you catch it? The first part of the armor we are encouraged to put on is "the belt of truth." God's Word is the truth. This is not just for today but for thousands of years gone by. Let's go back when God was very patient with the Israelites. This scenario depicted one of His divine attributes, also known as longsuffering. God waited until the Israelites' children got to be young adults. He wanted young warriors that would be obedient to the new leader, named Joshua, whom He raised up. The book of Joshua was written by Joshua who God used to lead these young warriors into the Promised Land. This is what is stated in the very beginning of that book: "Do not let this Book of the Law depart from your mouth; meditate on it day and night, so that you may be careful to do everything written in it. Then you will be prosperous and successful" (Jos. 1:8). Do you want to be prosperous and successful? That is the spiritual recipe.

Next, Joshua instructs the young warriors that God is going to use them to possess the land. He informs them: "Do not give a war cry, do not raise your voices, do not say a word until the day I tell you to shout. Then shout" (Jos. 6:10). Joshua commands them "do not say a word until the day I tell you." That right there is a key verse that can be used when discussing the spiritual disciplines of solitude and silence. That's powerful!

We are talking about the warfare of the believer. The Israelites that came out of Egypt didn't want to be disciplined and listen to God's voice. The book of Joshua informs us: "The Israelites had moved about in the desert forty years until all the men who were of military age when they left Egypt had died, since they had not obeyed the Lord. For the Lord had sworn to them that they would not see the land that He had solemnly promised their fathers to give us, a land flowing with milk and honey. So He raised up their sons in their place, and these were the ones Joshua circumcised. They were still uncircumcised because they had not been circumcised on the way. And after the whole nation had been circumcised, they remained where they were in camp until they were healed" (Jos. 5:6-8).

Their fathers did not want to be disciplined in the wilderness. The wonderful book of Hebrews informs me, "Do not regard lightly the discipline of the Lord, nor faint when you are reproved by Him; for those whom the Lord loves He disciplines, and He scourges every son whom He receives" (Heb. 12:5-6). In fact, God's Word speaks many powerful scriptures regarding discipline. Let me park here for a minute. I want to lay a foundation built on Scripture. The infallible Word informs us, "Know then in your heart that as a man disciplines his son, so the Lord your God disciplines you" (Dt. 8:5). "Does He who disciplines nations not punish? Does He who teaches man lack knowledge" (Ps. 94:10)? "Our fathers disciplined us for a little while as they thought best; but God disciplines us for our good, that we may share in His holiness" (Heb. 12:10). "He openeth also their ear to discipline, and commandeth that they return from iniquity" (Job 36:10 KJV). And then: "But those who suffer He delivers in their suffering; He speaks to them in their affliction" (Job 36:15).

As you probably noticed by now I have quoted many verses from the book of Joshua and Ephesians. The book of Joshua is the warfare book in the Old Testament and the book of Ephesians is the warfare book in the New Testament.

Throughout this compilation, my purpose is to keep challenging you with different spiritual disciplines, many of which you may want to rededicate yourself to, or double-up your daily activity with.

Let's hear what the Bible says regarding meditating in God's Word. "For the word of God is living and active. Sharper than any double-edged sword, it penetrates even to dividing soul and spirit, joints and marrow; it judges the thoughts and attitudes of the heart" (Heb. 4:12). "If you continue in My word, then you are truly disciples of Mine; and you will know the truth, and the truth will make you free" (Jn. 8:31). "Your Word, O Lord, is eternal; it stands firm in the heavens" (Ps. 119:89). "My covenant will I not break, nor alter the thing that is gone out of My lips" (Ps. 89:34). "Faith comes by hearing and hearing by the Word of God" (Ro. 10:17). This is what Jeremiah says regarding God's Word: "In my heart it becomes like a burning fire shut up in my bones and I am weary of holding it in, and I cannot endure it" (Jer. 20:9 NASB).

Discipline #2 – Prayer

I heard a powerful man of God by the name of Leonard Ravenhill state in a sermon, "You can tell a man by his prayer life." While I was ministering life at the Salvation Army in Providence, RI, I would always challenge the crowd. I would ask them how much time they spent in prayer and in God's Word. Many would inform me they spent about fifteen minutes. I would then ask them how much time they spent watching television. Many would say several hours. Then I would ask them if they loved the television twelve times more than they loved Jesus and prayer.

The Bible says: "In the same way, the Spirit helps us in our weakness. We do not know what we ought to pray for, but the Spirit Himself intercedes for us with groans that words cannot express. And He who searches our hearts knows the mind of the Spirit, because the Spirit intercedes for the saints in accordance with God's will" (Ro.8:26-27). Then Jesus' brother Jude states in the book of Jude, "But you, dear friends, build yourselves up in your most holy faith and pray in the Holy Spirit. Keep yourselves in God's love as you wait for the mercy of our Lord Jesus Christ to bring you to eternal life" (Jude 20-21). We keep ourselves in God's love, praying in the Spirit. Now that's powerful. In fact, the Apostle Paul stated, "I pray that you, being rooted and established in love, may have power, together with all the saints, to grasp how wide and long and high and deep is the love of Christ, and to know this love that surpasses knowledge—that you may be filled to the measure of all the fullness of God" (Eph. 3:17-19). Therefore, keeping ourselves in the love of Christ is the full measure of the Father.

Discipline #3 – Fasting

I should write a book on fasting. I do not know one person, and may go through my entire life without meeting an individual, who fasts as much as I do. I like to fast. I don't inform people of this because I do it unto God. Almost all of the major breakthroughs that I have experienced have been while on a long fast. It is a way of life for me. I truly enjoy it.

As Christians we have to position ourselves spiritually so the Lord can bless us due to our faith, obedience, spiritual hunger and maturity through prayer, fasting, feasting on God's Word, and other spiritual disciplines we incorporate. I have heard people say that Jesus really does inform the church to fast. Well, He didn't have to. They were living a lifestyle of prayer and fasting. That's one of the main reasons I believe the early church turned the world upside down. Jesus stated often: "When you fast..." That word "when" implies that they were already fasting.

I often think of Anna, the prophetess of the early church. Luke states this about her: "She was very old; she had lived with her husband seven years after her marriage, and then was a widow until she was eighty-four. She never left the temple but worshiped night and day, fasting and praying. Coming up to them at that very moment, she gave thanks to God and spoke about the child to all who were looking forward to the redemption of Jerusalem" (Lk. 2:36-38). She was eighty-four, fasted and prayed day and night, and never left the temple. That's very powerful. I will certainly be discussing more on the topic of fasting in other chapters.

Discipline #4 – Study

I have to laugh when I think about this discipline. A pastor from Texas took me out for lunch an hour ago. I was informing him how I had every piece of paper from fifty-two classes from Zion Bible College. However, I stored them in a basement and they all got contaminated with mold and mildew. I spent a whole week copying every piece of paper and then scanning them so that I have them in hard copy and in a scanned copy. Why all this work? Because Jesus said, "Be diligent to present yourself approved to God as a workman who does not need to be ashamed, accurately handling the word of truth" (2 Tim. 2:15). I need to be a good steward and take care of everything God has put in my possession. My studies have blessed me, to be a blessing to others, all for the glory of God. Another verse in the book of Second Timothy informs me, "All scripture is inspired by God and profitable for teaching, for reproof, for correction, for training in righteousness; so that the man of God may be adequate, equipped for every good work" (2 Tim. 3:16-17).

I need to study so I can give proper instruction. Pastors, teachers, prophets, and evangelist must feed the sheep. The books of First and Second Timothy are Pastoral Epistles. Listen to the next verse: "I solemnly charge you in the presence of God and of Christ Jesus, who is to judge the living and the dead, and by His appearing and His kingdom: preach the Word; be ready in season and out of season; reprove, rebuke, exhort, with great patience and instruction. For the time will come when they will not endure sound doctrine; but wanting to have their ears tickled, they will accumulate for themselves teachers in accordance to their own desires, and will turn away their ears from the truth and will turn aside to myths" (2 Tim. 2-4).

My question to the saints is, what are you listening to? What are you studying? Are you studying the stock market or your favorite sports team? Are you listening to the news on the television or God's Word? What are you listening to and what are you studying?

Discipline #5 – Simplicity

This is one of my favorites. Because I have let spiritual disciplines change me, I am able to live a life of simplicity. While ministering in Reynosa, Mexico every week, I can tell how a life of simplicity has changed the Mexican people tremendously. They are so sensitive and open because of the lifestyle they live.

Spiritual Disciplines

All they do is look at me and the fire of God ignites their hearts and minds. I don't have to lay hands on them or pray for them I just look at them and down they go under the power of God. It certainly has nothing to do with me. However, it has everything to do with their lifestyle of simplicity. There is an old saying; "The more you have, the more it has you." Some nights the worship team would only get to the second song before the band members were on the floor under the power of God. An individual contacted me and informed me of the many gun battles that were taking place in Reynosa. I informed him it wasn't the gun battles that were hindering me from going into Reynosa. It was that the armor bearer, Antonio, would get drunk in the Holy Ghost and was unable to drive the truck. One week he only made it four blocks from the church and we had to wait a half an hour for him to sober up. A life of simplicity is a powerful tool against the Kingdom of darkness. What Antonio and I want is simple. We want more of God!

Discipline #6 – Solitude

For me, solitude and silence go hand in hand to a degree. When I am fasting, especially when I am starting a fast, (the first three or four days) I practice these disciplines even more. The more you dwell in the secret place of the Most High the more you allow this discipline to take hold of you. Mental, emotional and physical attachments impinge upon your devotion to Christ.

We must not compromise with distracting mindsets but must remember this key scripture: "Finally, brothers, whatever is true, whatever is noble, whatever is right, whatever is pure, whatever is lovely, whatever is admirable—if anything is excellent or praiseworthy—think about such things" (Phil. 4:8). We must "take captive every thought to make it obedient to Christ" (2 Cor. 10:5).

We must not compromise. Let me inform you what compromise means. It means: "to cause the impairment of." Impaired means: "being in less than perfect or whole condition." I must also remember sin is the loss of God's best for me. May I give you my favorite scripture regarding simplicity? Saint Paul wrote it on his third missionary journey around 57 AD. He stated: "For I am jealous for you with a godly jealousy; for I betrothed you to one husband, so that to Christ I might present you as a pure virgin. But I am afraid that, as the serpent deceived Eve by his craftiness, your minds will be led astray from the simplicity and purity of devotion to Christ" (2 Cor. 11:2-3).

Simplicity and purity of devotion to Christ are keys to having life and having it abundantly.

Discipline #7 – Submission

The purposes of practicing the spiritual disciplines are so we can be free. "The purpose of the discipline is freedom. Our aim is the freedom, not the discipline. The moment we make the discipline our central focus, we turn it into law and lose the corresponding freedom. The liberation is the end: the disciplines are merely the means."[1]

Let's see what Jesus has to say regarding submission: "Then He called the crowd to Him along

---

[1] Richard J. Foster, *Celebration of Discipline* (New York: HarperCollins Publishers Inc. 1978), 114.

with His disciples and said: "If anyone would come after Me, he must deny himself and take up his cross and follow Me. For whoever wants to save his life will lose it, but whoever loses his life for Me and for the gospel will save it" (Mk. 8:34-35). "Jesus made it quite clear that self-denial is the only way to love ourselves. Self-denial is the touchstone for the discipline of submission."[2] After all, isn't the cross a sign of submission?

Discipline #8 – Service

I am not breaking each discipline down powerfully like the many books available to you can. I am merely informing you how they have blessed my life and why I practice them. I am attempting to challenge you to move deeper toward them. I am also challenging myself. When I write books, I remember incidents that I have completely forgotten about until I write on that subject matter. I highly recommend you buy Foster's book and get blessed by it. These are life changing subject matters that will enrich our heavenly calling so we can be a blessing to others.

In my last month at Bible College, the guys decided to have a foot washing service. No one washed my feet, however, I was asked to wash a couple of gentlemen's feet. I can tell you it was a very humbling experience for me. I truly believe that many times when I used to get depressed it was because I had my mind on myself. My mind is often self-centered. After I would serve someone else or witness to someone, peace would come. Service is powerful. Even Jesus Himself said: "The Son of Man did not come to be

---

[2] Ibid, 115.

served, but to serve, and to give His life as a ransom for many" (Mt. 20:28).

Discipline #9 – Confession

The Lord Jesus Christ has left the church with two ordinances, Water Baptism and the Lord's Table. An ordinance means: "A command of the Lord." The church is commanded to water baptize believers and to take communion (The Lord's Table). Jesus made this statement regarding communion: "Do this in remembrance of Me" (1 Cor. 11:24). The Israelites would celebrate many week long feasts throughout the year reflecting on what God had done in their lives. General busyness of the present day has a tendency to steal from this practice. Be careful not to lose focus on what the Lord considers vital.

One of the most powerful ways to reflect on God is during communion. Jesus stated; "Do this in remembrance of Me." The bread represents His body. It represents His provision—what He did for us at the cross; what He's doing right now by way of sanctification through the Holy Spirit; and lastly, what He's going to do by coming back for the Church. The cup represents the blood of Christ at Calvary. The cup crushes demons, poverty, sickness, every curse along with anything and everything that is affiliated with the kingdom of darkness. That's powerful. There is power in the blood!

I consider every communion service, whether taken at church with the saints or alone in my office, a healing service. I recall one morning about six months ago when I woke up and felt very sick. I was having trouble breathing along with pains in my chest and throughout my entire body. I thought, "There is no way I can make it to class today." Do you know the devil is a liar? I went into the refrigerator, took a piece of bread and a small cup of grape juice. I said, "Father please bless these symbols that represent the body and blood of Jesus. I confess every sin and I thank you Father that I can enter this healing service by the blood of the Lamb." I reflected on what Jesus did for me, what He is doing now and what He's going to do. Within five minutes, I was dancing around my kitchen table to the song "The Spirit of the Lord Is on Me." Glory to God! I went to school and gave that powerful testimony.

The Holy Bible says, "And there was war in heaven. Michael and his angels fought against the dragon, and the dragon and his angels fought back. But he was not strong enough, and they lost their place in heaven. The great dragon was hurled down—that ancient serpent called the devil, or Satan, who leads the whole world astray. He was hurled to the earth, and his angels with him. Then I heard a loud voice in heaven say: 'Now have come the salvation and the power and the kingdom of our God, and the authority of His Christ. For the accuser of our brothers, who accuses them before our God day and night, has been hurled down. They overcame him by the blood of the Lamb and by the word of their testimony'" (Rev. 12:7-11).

Discipline #10 – Worship

The Lord has increased my knowledge of the importance of worship this year. I drove to San Antonio, Texas in January of 2010 and attended a weekend long Benny Hinn conference. Benny Hinn is a professional worshipper. Worship brings in the anointing. This is why individuals got up out of wheelchairs and started walking. The anointing was so strong in those services.

I personally believe the reason the Spanish churches are growing much faster than the American churches in the United States is because they worship much longer, which draws in the anointing. I refuse to put a turkey in the oven before going to a Spanish service because I do not know for sure if the service will end the same day. They are in no hurry. They just flow with the anointing.

It's important to note that, "Believers can truly worship only with the help of the Spirit of truth who sanctifies and illuminates them by means of the truth of God's Word--the truth about God and the truth about humans, their sin and salvation. In true worship there is an encounter with God for which God must make man capable by His grace."[3]

Some key scriptures regarding worship are: "Therefore, I urge you, brothers, in view of God's mercy, to offer your bodies as living sacrifices, holy and pleasing to God—this is your spiritual act of worship. Do not conform any longer to the pattern of this world, but be transformed by the renewing of your mind. Then you will be able to test and approve what God's will is—His good, pleasing and perfect will" (Ro. 12:1-2).

One of my favorite scriptures regarding worship is: "And I saw what looked like a sea of glass mixed with fire and, standing beside the sea, those who had been victorious over the beast and his image and over the number of his name. They held harps

---

[3] R. Schnackenburg, *The Gospel According to St. John, I* (New York: Herder & Herder 1968), 437.

given them by God and sang the song of Moses the servant of God and the song of the Lamb: Great and marvelous are Your deeds, Lord God Almighty. Just and true are Your ways, King of the ages. Who will not fear You, O Lord, and bring glory to Your name? For You alone are holy. All nations will come and worship before You, for your righteous acts have been revealed" (Rev. 15:2-4).

Now I would like to discuss my favorite part of worship. We worship God with tithes and offerings. Wait! Don't get up to get a drink. The Lord wants to talk to you. I heard a pastor state on Sunday that the church he was pastoring needed additional individuals to serve in the church. He stated, "Twenty percent of the people do eighty percent of the work and twenty percent give eighty percent of the finances." That is very sad and it also explains to me why many individuals do not have life in abundance in every area of their life.

Discipline #11 – Guidance

It is important for me to look back at history and make sure I don't make the same mistakes that other people did. From history we know: "God led the children of Israel out of bondage *as a people*. The people, however, soon found God's unmediated presence too awful, too glorious and begged, 'Let not God speak to us, lest we die'" (Exod. 20:19). So Moses became their mediator. We also know a day came when Israel rejected even the prophet in favor of a king. From that point on the prophet was the outsider. He was a lonely voice crying in the wilderness;

sometimes obeyed, sometimes killed, but almost always on the outside."[4]

Thank God for the finished work at Calvary by the Lord Jesus. God then could and did send the Holy Spirit. We all need to allow God to have His way in every area of our life. We can have abundant life in every area if we submit completely to the Holy Spirit. The Bible declares, "But the Counselor, the Holy Spirit, whom the Father will send in my name, will teach you all things and will remind you of everything I have said to you" (Jn. 14:26). Also a very powerful scripture regarding guidance is, "As for you, the anointing you received from Him remains in you, and you do not need anyone to teach you. But as His anointing teaches you about all things and as that anointing is real, not counterfeit—just as it has taught you, remain in Him" (1 Jn. 2:27).

My favorite section of the Bible that ministers to my heart the most regarding God's guidance is Psalm twenty-three. I would like to close out this topic with this Psalm.

The Lord, the Psalmist's Shepherd

"The Lord is my shepherd; I shall not be in want. He makes me lie down in green pastures, He leads me beside quiet waters, He restores my soul. He guides me in paths of righteousness for His name's sake. Even though I walk through the valley of the shadow of death, I will fear no evil, for You are with me; Your rod and Your staff, they comfort me. You prepare a table before me in the presence of my

---

[4] Richard J. Foster, *Celebration of Disciplines* (New York: HarperCollins Publishers Inc. 1978), 176.

enemies. You anoint my head with oil; my cup overflows. Surely goodness and love will follow me all the days of my life, and I will dwell in the house of the Lord forever" (Psalm 23:1-6).

Discipline #12 – Celebration

Rejoicing and celebration brings much satisfaction. We must realize that the God of heaven and earth cares and provides for His people. Rejoicing and celebration strengthens us. The Bible says, "Do not grieve, for the joy of the Lord is your strength" (Ne. 8:10). Without a joyful Spirit, pressing forward in the things of God becomes a difficult grind. That is not how it should be.

Joy is one of the many fruits of the Spirit (see Gal. 5:22). Joy produces strength, and zeal. For me personally, without joy, strength and zeal, there is no contentment. Celebration is a must. Paul wrote to Timothy and said, "Godliness with contentment is great gain" (1 Tim. 6:6). Let's not forget the powerful scripture that informs us to: "Rejoice in the Lord always. I will say it again: Rejoice" (Phil. 4:4)!

WHAT ARE YOU WAITING FOR?

Saints of God, we all need to rise up and become experts in the spiritual equipment with which God has lavished us. There is a sick and dying world out there that needs a touch from heaven and God wants to use us as instruments to touch them. Below is a list of some of the spiritual equipment that is at our disposal. We do not have to go through twelve steps or seven steps. One step is required and that's to step in.

Faith – Faith and the Word of God are the only things that will allow us to roll over the kingdom of darkness. And faith comes by hearing and by hearing the Word of God.

The Word of God – "For the Word of God is living and active. Sharper than any double-edged sword, it penetrates even to dividing soul and spirit, joints and marrow; it judges the thoughts and attitudes of the heart" (Heb. 4:12).

The Holy Spirit – "But the Counselor, the Holy Spirit, whom the Father will send in my name, will teach you all things and will remind you of everything I have said to you" (Jn. 14:26). Another scripture is, "As for you, the anointing you received from Him remains in you, and you do not need anyone to teach you. But as His anointing teaches you about all things and as that anointing is real, not counterfeit—just as it has taught you, remain in Him" (1 Jn. 2:27). The following is a list of some of the things the Holy Spirit is involved with. Assuring, baptizing, comforting, confronting, convicting, empowering, filling, gifting, guiding, healing, indwelling, interceding, praying, refining, regenerating, sealing, teaching, and uniting to name some of them.

Angels – "The angel of the Lord encamps around those who fear him, and he delivers them" (Ps. 34:7). Also, "Are not all angels ministering spirits sent to serve those who will inherit salvation" (Heb. 1:14)?

Other Saints – "As iron sharpens iron, so one man sharpens another" (Pr. 27:17).

Gifts from the Father – "We have different gifts, according to the grace given us. If a man's gift is prophesying, let him use it in proportion to his faith. If it is serving, let him serve; if it is teaching, let him teach; if it is encouraging, let him encourage; if it is contributing to the needs of others, let him give generously; if it is leadership, let him govern diligently; if it is showing mercy, let him do it cheerfully" (Ro. 12:6-8).

Gifts from the Son – "It was He who gave some to be apostles, some to be prophets, some to be evangelists, and some to be pastors and teachers" (Eph. 4:11).

Gifts from the Holy Spirit – "There are different kinds of gifts, but the same Spirit. There are different kinds of service, but the same Lord. There are different kinds of working, but the same God works all of them in all men. Now to each one the manifestation of the Spirit is given for the common good. To one there is given through the Spirit the message of wisdom, to another the message of knowledge by means of the same Spirit, to another faith by the same Spirit, to another gifts of healing by that one Spirit, to another miraculous powers, to another prophecy, to another distinguishing between spirits, to another speaking in different kinds of tongues, and to still another the interpretation of tongues. All these are the work of one and the same Spirit, and He gives them to each one, just as He determines" (1 Cor. 12:4-11).

God's Love – "And hope does not disappoint us, because God has poured out His love into our hearts by the Holy Spirit, whom He has given us" (Ro. 5:5). Also, "Love never fails" (1 Cor. 13:8). Lastly, "Faith which worketh by love" (Gal. 5:6 KJV).

Power to Witness – "But you will receive power when the Holy Spirit comes on you; and you will be My witnesses in Jerusalem, and in all Judea and Samaria, and to the ends of the earth" (Acts 1:8).

Authority – "I have given you authority to trample on snakes and scorpions and to overcome all the power of the enemy; nothing will harm you" (Lk. 10:19).

The Name Jesus – When you say the name Jesus every demon trembles. Everything has to bow to that name.

The Blood of Jesus – You can bleed the blood of Jesus over every situation. There is power in the blood.

What Are You Waiting For

The Law of the Spirit of Life vs. The Law of Sin and Death

The Bible says, "For the law of the Spirit of life in Christ Jesus hath made me free from the law of sin and death" (Ro. 8:2). When you're born-again you become a new species of being. "As you begin to live out your Christian walk the law of the Spirit of life in Christ Jesus starts to operate in your life. As you pray, walk in love, live by faith, manifest the fruits of the spirit these all function using the law of the Spirit of life in Jesus Christ.

Anything contrary is from the kingdom of darkness. Sin, sickness, disease, poverty, and death are all characteristics of the curse, and function according to the law of sin and death (see Romans 8). "The law of sin and death includes fear—fear in the ability of things to hurt you, fear of animals, fear of people and fear of the weather, to name a few. Fix your mind on Jesus, believe and speak God's Word, and fear of death will begin to shrink."[5]

The Law of Faith

Understanding God's law of faith will produce results. "Whatever you say and believe without doubting, you can have! Whosoever means this spiritual law of faith will work for anyone who uses it (see Mark 11:23). You can cause your faith to grow and get stronger by studying and believing God's Word. Every time you hear the Word, faith comes (see Romans 10:17). To produce results, faith must be

---

[5] Kenneth Copeland, Believer's Voice of Victory Broadcast Notes, Teaching titled, *Faith in the Love of God Brings Results*, February 11-15, 2019, p. 1.

spoken. What you believe in your heart is what you'll speak, so speak faith."[6]

The Law of Sowing and Reaping

In the Bible seed refers to our words and our money. We can sow words (seeds) of life or words (seeds) of death. The Bible says, "Death and life are in the power of the tongue: and they that love it shall eat the fruit thereof" (Pr. 18:21). It also says, "Be not deceived; God is not mocked: for whatsoever a man soweth, that shall he also reap" (Gal. 6:7).

Now let's look at money as seed. Regarding us sowing money the Bible says, "But this I say, He which soweth sparingly shall reap also sparingly; and he which soweth bountifully shall reap also bountifully" (2 Cor. 9:6).

---

[6] Ibid, 2.

WHEN TO ENGAGE DISCIPLINES

When Did Jesus Have His Devotional Life?

1. In the mornings (Mark 1:35)
2. In the afternoons (Matthew 14:22)
3. In the evenings (Luke 6:12)

Scriptures Regarding Our Devotional Life

1. Mornings (Ps. 1:2, 5:3, 88:1, 13 and Dan. 6:10)
2. Afternoons (Ps. 88:1, Dan. 6:10, and Acts 10:39)
3. Evenings (Ps. 1:2, 4:4, 6:6, 63:6, 88:1 and Dan. 6:10)

What Conclusion Can We Draw?

1. Anytime is alright with God.
2. We do not need to be locked into a specific time.
3. What works best in my life?
4. We must always be open to God's prompting.
5. We cannot be legalistic.

I WANT TO CHALLENGE YOU

I remember times when individuals from Bible College would be up by the altar before, during and after chapel service. When led by the Spirit, I would go up to pray with them and they would say things like, "I want God to use me more" or "I'm seeking God to move in my life." I would lay hands on them and ask God to give them spiritual hunger to set their alarm clocks one hour earlier.

The Bible says, "But seek first His kingdom and His righteousness, and all these things will be given to you as well" (Mt. 6:33). It doesn't say, "Set your alarm clock for 7:30 am, get up, brush your teeth, spend five minutes with God, get to class at 8:05 and God will use you and move in every area of your life." What time is your alarm clock set for?

My challenge to you is scriptural. The Bible says: "I love them that love me; and those that seek me early shall find me" (Pr. 8:17 KJV). Are baseball games or other television programs keeping you up late at night, which in turn affects your devotion to the Lord when morning comes?

EPHESIANS IS VITAL

It is vital to study and understand the book of Ephesians in order to be equipped with resources and combat the warfare fronts of the world, the flesh, and the demonic. We must take every word and apply it in our daily walk in and with Christ. Wisdom is the proper application of knowledge. Jesus Himself stated: "But everyone who hears these words of mine and does not put them into practice is like a foolish man who built his house on sand" (Mt. 7:26).

Can you imagine hanging out with Saint Paul back in the day for three years and allowing him to teach and train you? Wouldn't that be awesome? He was one of the greatest minds western civilization has ever seen. Well the people of Ephesus had the opportunity to do just that. Paul was there longer than anywhere else. They got to break bread with him and hang out.

After being with them for three whole years, guess what Paul had to share with them? He says: "I know that after I leave, savage wolves will come in among you and will not spare the flock" (Acts 20:29). It appears they may need Paul to write a book to equip them for warfare. Paul was a seasoned apostle with a pastor's heart, so that is just what Paul did.

Let's look at the next couple of verses which state: "Even from your own number men will arise and distort the truth in order to draw away disciples after them. So be on your guard! Remember that for three years I never stopped warning each of you night and day with tears" (Acts 20:30-31). With that in mind let's look to the book of Ephesians to see exactly how Paul equips them with instruction for warfare.

Ephesians is Vital

He begins in chapter one wasting no time. "Praise be to the God and Father of our Lord Jesus Christ, who has blessed us in the heavenly realms with every spiritual blessing in Christ" (Eph. 1:3). This enforces what he states in chapter two that we are seated in heavenly places in Christ. These next scriptures are tremendous. He writes: "In Him we have redemption through His blood, the forgiveness of sins, in accordance with the riches of God's grace that He lavished on us with all wisdom and understanding" (Eph. 1:7-8). "In Him we were also chosen, having been predestined according to the plan of Him who works out everything in conformity with the purpose of His will, in order that we, who were the first to hope in Christ, might be for the praise of His glory. And you also were included in Christ when you heard the word of truth, the gospel of your salvation. Having believed, you were marked in Him with a seal, the promised Holy Spirit, who is a deposit guaranteeing our inheritance until the redemption of those who are God's possession—to the praise of His glory" (Eph. 1:11-14).

If you notice in those verses Paul mentions many times the term: "In Him." In the New Testament the terms, "In Christ," "In Him," and "In Whom" are used about 150-170 times depending on the version. It's important that we learn our position in Christ in these first two chapters. I cut and pasted all those verses that state: 'In Him" and I meditate on them some mornings. They are very powerful!

In chapter one we learn: "That power is like the working of His mighty strength, which He exerted in Christ when He raised Him from the dead and seated Him at His right hand in the heavenly realms, far above all rule and authority, power and dominion, and every title that can be given, not only in the present age but also in the one to come" (Eph. 1:19-21). Jesus is seated in heaven with God; we also are. Let's look at chapter two. It states: "But because of His great love for us, God, who is rich in mercy, made us alive with Christ even when we were dead in transgressions — it is by grace you have been saved. And God raised us up with Christ and seated us with Him in the heavenly realms in Christ Jesus" (Eph. 2:4-6). So not only are we "In Christ" but we are seated in heavenly places "In Christ." If we are "In Christ" that means that all of my being which includes relationships, finances and everything else is "In Christ."

Before I go to preach I have to be seated with Christ. Before I go cast out demons I have to be seated with Christ. I am called to be with Christ — that is my calling. Let's look in the book of Mark and investigate when Jesus appointed the twelve apostles. It says: "He appointed twelve — designating them apostles — that they might be with Him and that He might send them out to preach and to have authority to drive out demons" (Mk. 3:14-15). They weren't called to preach and cast out demons. They were called to be with Him. Only then would He send them out.

Chapters three, four, five and six discuss walking in love and taking a stand against the wiles of the devil. We cannot walk in love without sitting first. We can not take a stand without sitting first. We sit, then walk and stand. There is a five dollar book titled: *Sit, Walk and Stand* by Watchman Nee. It will bless you if you purchase this item and study it.

Let's go to the Bible to see what the book of Ephesians says about the walk of the believer. The NASB version uses many more verses regarding this subject so I will be using those scriptures. Remember we have to sit in Christ first so we can walk, right?

The Bible informs us: "You formerly walked according to the course of this world, according to the prince of the power of the air, of the spirit that is now working in the sons of disobedience" (Eph. 2:2). "For we are His workmanship, created in Christ Jesus for good works, which God prepared beforehand so that we would walk in them" (Eph. 2:10). "Therefore I, the prisoner of the Lord, implore you to walk in a manner worthy of the calling with which you have been called" (Eph. 4:1). "So this I say, and affirm together with the Lord, that you walk no longer just as the Gentiles also walk, in the futility of their mind" (Eph. 4:17). "Walk in love, just as Christ also loved you and gave Himself up for us, an offering and a sacrifice to God as a fragrant aroma" (Eph. 5:2). "You were formerly darkness, but now you are Light in the Lord; walk as children of Light" (Eph. 5:8). And lastly: "Therefore be careful how you walk, not as unwise men but as wise" (Eph. 5:15).

Are you drawing a conclusion that the book of Ephesians is vital? Paul wants to equip the believers because of the savage wolves. He is trying to "dewolve" them. Amen! I truly liked Watchmen Nee's input on this subject. T.D. Jakes also breaks this down with excellence. He states: "When you know your position you can overcome your condition." He goes on further discussing the walk, wealth, worship, workmanship and warfare of the believer. In Ephesians chapter six it discusses "the armor of God." Let's see what God is saying: "Put on the full armor of God so that you can take your stand against the devil's schemes" (Eph.6:11). "Therefore put on the full armor of God, so that when the day of evil comes, you may be able to stand your ground, and after you have done everything, to stand" (Eph. 6:13). "Stand firm then, with the belt of truth buckled around your waist, with the breastplate of righteousness in place" (Eph. 6:14). In these last days, you will have to brace up and stand firm in faith. Faith is the only thing that will get you through.

IN CHRIST

I intend to prove that everything an individual needs that pertains to life and godliness in this world and the one to come is found in Christ. I love feeling blessed and being blessed, that's why I enjoy the following verse so much. It reminds me how blessed I am and why. "Blessed be the God and Father of our Lord Jesus Christ, who has blessed us with every spiritual blessing in the heavenly places in Christ, just as He chose us in Him before the foundation of the world, that we would be holy and blameless before Him" (Eph. 1:3-4). Has blessed us, meaning everything is finished. Receive whatever you need by faith right now. Faith is always right now.

"Christian faith and life have their center in God's Son and the Epistle therefore opens with an expression of gratitude for all that is found in Him. Paul traces 'every spiritual blessing' to its ultimate source in the eternal purpose of God. Christians were selected in Christ prior to the work of creation."[7] Paul informs us: "But by His doing you are in Christ Jesus, who became to us wisdom from God, and righteousness and sanctification, and redemption..." (1 Cor. 1:30). That makes me want to shout!

Immediately after the fall of man the Lord God said to the serpent: "And I will put enmity between you and the woman, and between your seed and her seed; He shall bruise you on the head, and you shall bruise Him on the heel" (Gen. 3:15).

---

[7] A. Skevington Wood, *The Expositor's Bible Commentary* (Grand Rapids: Zondervan, 1981), 23.

In Christ

This is the first prophecy mentioned in the infallible Word of God. "But when the fullness of time came, God sent forth His Son, born of a woman, born under the Law, so that He might redeem those who were under the Law, that we might receive adoption as sons. Because you are sons, God has sent forth the Spirit of His Son into our hearts, crying, Abba! Father! Therefore you are no longer a slave, but a son; and if a son, then an heir through God" (Gal. 4:4-7). "For as in Adam all die, so in Christ all will be made alive" (1 Cor. 15:22).

God's servant Jeremiah prophesied regarding a new covenant stating: "Behold, days are coming, declares the Lord, when I will make a new covenant with the house of Israel and with the house of Judah, not like the covenant which I made with their fathers in the day that I took them by the hand to bring them out of the land of Egypt, My covenant which I broke, although I was a husband to them, declares the Lord. But this is the covenant which I will make with the house of Israel after those days, declares the Lord, I will put My law within them and on their heart I will write it; and I will be their God, and they shall be My people" (Jer. 31:31-33). This is indicative of what Christ has done for us.

Sanctified in Christ Jesus

When Paul addresses the Corinthian church he writes: "To the church of God which is at Corinth, to those who have been sanctified in Christ Jesus…" (1 Cor. 1:2). As part of the sanctification process Paul informs us that a process of 'putting on the new man' is indispensable. He informs the saints: "Let the word of Christ richly dwell within you…" (Col. 3:16) and do not be conformed to this world, but be transformed by the renewing of your mind, so that you may prove what the will of God is, that which is good and acceptable and perfect" (Ro. 12:2). To be sanctified in Christ involves much devotion time spent in God's Word. Paul tells us: "work out your salvation with fear and trembling; for it is God who is at work in you, both to will and to work for His good pleasure" (Phil. 2:12). We work out our salvation in this eschatological tension. "He who overcomes, I will make him a pillar in the temple of My God, and he will not go out from it anymore, and I will write on him the name of My God, and the name of the city of My God, the new Jerusalem, which comes down out of heaven from My God, and My new name" (Rev. 3:12).

Veil Lifted When in Christ

The Apostle Paul, one of the greatest minds in western civilization writes masterfully by informing us: "their minds were made dull; for to this day the same veil remains when the old covenant is read. It has been removed, because only in Christ is it taken away" (2 Cor. 3:14). "A veil covered their hearts comparable to the veil that covered Moses face. Paul could call it the 'same' veil, because in both cases a veil prevented vision, whether physical or spiritual. This veil remained unlifted in the case of the unbelieving Jew, because only as he came to be 'in Christ' was the veil set aside."[8]

---

[8] Ibid, 337.

In Christ

Our Position in Christ

I feel the backbone to every Christian's walk with God is the conclusions he or she draws regarding their position in Christ. This is why I constantly urge individuals to meditate (*lectio divina*) on the book of Ephesians verses 1:1-3:31. The key verses regarding the aforementioned are: "But God, being rich in mercy, because of His great love with which He loved us, even when we were dead in our transgressions, made us alive together with Christ (by grace you have been saved), and raised us up with Him, and seated us with Him in heavenly places in Christ Jesus, so that the ages to come He might show the surpassing riches of His grace in kindness toward us in Christ Jesus" (Eph. 2:4-7). By having firm bedrock regarding this position, Christians will prevent the dark forces of this world from tossing them to and fro.

In the Spirit / In Christ

If Christians have a deep revelation of who they are in Christ Jesus, when the hot winds of testing blow they "…will be like a tree firmly planted by steams of water, which yields its fruit in its season and its leaf does not wither; and whatever he does, he prospers" (Ps. 1:3). *Whatever, he does, he prospers.* A Christian "does not need others to tell him, he needs no code of morals. He can decide for himself what his course of action should be. He is 'Christ-autonomous,' or, in a phrase more familiar to us, he is 'the man in Christ.'

In Christ

The freedom of the Christian in his spiritual and moral life is 'in the Spirit' or 'in Christ.'"[9]

---

[9] Eric H. Wahlstrom, *The New Life in Christ (Philadelphia: Muhlenberg Press 1950), 152.*

THE HARMFUL EFFECTS OF LUST

When we understand lust and how it affects our lives, the more we will understand why we need a lifestyle of faith, fasting, studying, and prayer. Fasting will be discussed subsequently. When we fast, the Lord can undo the bonds of the yoke and by the anointing break every yoke (See Is. 58:6). As I went through the Bible, what arrested my attention was 1 Thessalonians 4:1-8 especially verse three. Verse three states: "For this is the will of God, your sanctification; that is, that you abstain from sexual immorality...." In the next verse we are informed: "...each of you know how to possess his own vessel in sanctification and honor, not in lustful passion..."

I know firsthand from my walk with God that "...each one is tempted when he is carried away and enticed by his own lust" (Jas. 1:14). I like what the Amplified Bible states: "But every person is tempted when he is drawn away, enticed and baited by his own evil desire. Then the evil desire, when it has conceived, gives birth to sin, and sin, when it is fully matured, brings forth death" (Jas. 1:14-15). I want to park here for a minute. Focus must be drawn to this word "conceive" in verse fifteen. It means to form or develop in the mind. Lust is a strong desire of any kind, more frequently in a bad sense. Lust is a longing that can never be satisfied or quenched. It keeps going and going until it gets into lascivious, which refers to: "unrestrained action" and/or "without boundaries." Then you have what the world calls addiction. The difference between good lust and bad lust is bad lust always strives for more. Lust says it's never enough.

The Harmful Effects of Lust

Desires can be fulfilled but lust cannot. Scriptures prove it is not quenchable. We must remember: "unrestrained thoughts produce unrestrained actions."

Proverbs 30:15 from the Amplified Bible reads: "The leech has two daughters, crying, give, give! There are three things that are never satisfied, yes, four that do not say, It is enough: Sheol (the place of the dead), the barren womb, the earth that is not satisfied with water, and the fire that says not, it is enough."

In First Thessalonians, in the first verse, we are told to: "…walk and please God (just as you actually walk), that you excel still more." It takes a combination of love and fear that brings obedience in order for us to excel. In his book *Knowledge of the Holy*, A.W. Tozer states: "When men no longer fear God, they transgress His laws without hesitation. The fear of consequences is no deterrent when the fear of God is gone."[10]

In verse six of 1 Thessalonians it states: "…the Lord is the avenger in all these things…." We must strive for perfection in Christ Jesus. Addictions, apart from the way and will of the Lord, bring setbacks and destruction. I love the following verse "See, I set before you today life and prosperity, death and destruction" (Deut. 30:15). We must choose life and prosperity. Obedience brings forth life which is vital to the sanctification process and purity. Lastly, "For God has not called us for the purpose of impurity, but in sanctification. So, he who rejects this is not rejecting man but the God who gives His Holy Spirit to you" (1 Thess. 4:7-8).

A powerful statement was once made by Augustine. He said, "Because my will was perverse it

---

[10] Tozer, W. Aiden, *The Knowledge of the Holy*. (New York: Harper Collins Publishers, 1961) 47.

changed to lust, and lust yielded to become habit, and habit not resisted became necessity."[11] That, I consider the recipe for addiction, and lust play's a major role. We need to be free from lust and addictions through a lifestyle of faith, study, prayer, fasting and obedience to God's Word. We must "take captive every thought to make it obedient to Christ" (2 Cor. 10:5). It's vital to understand that lust and addictions are detrimental and cause deception, delusion, destruction, distraction, delay, dissension, and death. Therefore, God's Word must dwell in us richly and we must make bold declarations of faith regarding every area of our life and ministry. We must run the devil out of town by faith!

---

[11] Francis J. Sheed, *Confessions by Augustine* (Indianapolis: Hackett Publishing 2007), 148.

STARTING A FAST

I touched on the topic of fasting in discipline #3, back when I discussed the twelve spiritual disciplines in chapter one. I guess I can best describe what I want to say like this: "When I first got saved, the Lord gave me a pistol. When I started serving as an usher, He gave me a rifle. When I got baptized in the Holy Ghost, He gave me a tank. When I got words of knowledge, He gave me a grenade. When He used me in the gift of healing, He gave me a B-52 bomber jet. However, when I fast, pray, and make bold declarations by faith, He gives me atomic bombs to use against Satan and his host. Prayer, fasting, and bold declarations of faith are very powerful. Fasting without prayer is not fasting, it is dieting. We must become experts with spiritual weapons."

Does God need to speak to me before I start a fast? Absolutely not! Fasting is a spiritual discipline; as is prayer. Do I need to hear from God before I pray? I believe I have made my point. I have noticed if you attempted to get church members to pray and fast, a small handful may show up. However, if you have something that involves food, everyone shows up with all the goods, cakes and pies included.

I like the article in the Providence Journal I read years ago by Stanley M. Aronson, M.D. titled *A brief history from gluttony to obesity*. He states: "Man is one of the few animals that eat when not hungry, drink when not thirsty, and have sex in all seasons, regardless of the need for offspring. Most people see food as one of the primary pleasures. Certainly, beyond its crucial role in nourishment, food is central to virtually every ritual. Births, commencements, weddings, anniversaries, retirements–even deaths–are each commemorated with a meal, with prescribed foods and libations."[12]

Fasting No Food – (Water Only)

Throughout this book, anything that is discussed regarding fasting will be referring to a fast without any food, just water. It's important I make that clear from the beginning. I really do not discuss fasting with many people and certainly do not tell people when I fast. I fast unto the Lord. I always commit the fast to Him. If I am somewhere while fasting and I get offered food I don't mention the word fasting. I tell them I decided not to eat today and pray instead. It eliminates having to hear all the nonsense.

Drinking a lot of water whether I am fasting or not is so important. I drink about two gallons of spring water a day. Every three months, during the first two days of a fast, I do a salt water flush. I take three 12 once glasses of lukewarm spring water and I put 1/3 of a tablespoon of sea salt in each one and drink them down. This flushes the colon and gets the fast going much faster. It's important not to do a salt water flush in the third day or more, also not more often than once every three months.

During the first three days, I also try to practice solitude and silence and put of a hedge around myself. I have been through this so many times and when it's time to fast, it's time to fast, and I need to use wisdom.

I also want to make sure that the day before I start the fast I didn't eat three big meals or go out to a

---

[12] Stanley M. Aronson, M.D., "A brief history from gluttony to obesity" Providence Journal 8 (September 2003) A9.

cookout and eat all day. I always try to make sure I eat light the day before I start the fast. It's not good to go from one extreme to the other. The most important part of the fast is breaking it, which I will be discussing.

Usually by the fifth day I get a breakthrough. Isaiah chapter 58 discusses fasting. This is how it describes a breakthrough: "Then your light shall break forth like the morning, your healing shall spring forth speedily, and your righteousness shall go before you; the glory of the Lord shall be your rear guard." (Is. 58:8 NKJV). That has always been my favorite scripture in the entire Bible. I have a book here in my library titled *The Name Book* by Dorothy Astoria. It states on the front cover: "Over 10,000 names, their meanings, origins, and spiritual significance." Here's what it says for my name Eugene:

Language / Culture Origin: Greek
Inherent Meaning: Born of Nobility
Spiritual Connotation: Vivacious
Scripture: Isaiah 58:8 NKJV

When I first started to live a lifestyle of fasting, it was good for me to have someone I could call and seek guidance and encouragement from. Sometimes you plan for people to encourage and assist you. Instead they hinder you. My favorite preacher stated, "Instead of praying for you, they prey on you."[13]

I remember I felt led to pray and fast for revival at Zion Bible College. I thought it would be much more powerful with another individual. So I started getting

---

[13] Bishop G. E. Patterson, *God Is with Us In Spite of Your Present Circumstances*, [sermon on-line] accessed 18 June, 2010; available from http://www.youtube.com/watch?v=zvmW0hWFuoE&feature=related

up every morning for a week to pray with another student with deep groaning. The Bible says: "In the same way the Spirit also helps our weakness; for we do not know how to pray as we should, but the Spirit Himself intercedes for us with groaning's too deep for words" (Ro. 8:26). Well after about the fourth morning meeting with him, because he wasn't fasting it seemed he was a hindrance rather than blessing. Then the Lord said to me: "I never told you to meet with him every morning." We must be led by the Lord in all things.

Prayer and fasting is very powerful especially when two individuals are both praying and fasting. Did you notice I said prayer and fasting? Fasting without prayer is not fasting, it is dieting. I truly hope and pray this is challenging you. I am grateful for the individuals that have challenged me over the years. I thank God for them.

DURING A FAST

It's vital you understand the following. "Fasting does not create faith. God's Word creates faith. "Faith comes by hearing and by hearing the Word of God" (Ro. 10:17). Fasting helps move your flesh out of the way. When you fast, you can see things you didn't see before. When you do it will bring the revelation you need to strengthen you for the battle."[14]

The more you understand what is going on with you during a fast, the easier it is to accept the many different discomforts that a fast will bring on. Our bodies are constantly being attacked by many different types of poisons. All day long we breathe it in. Foods from the local supermarkets are loaded with many different preservatives and drugs way too numerous to list. I wonder where the most drugs are located, in the supermarkets or the drug stores.

I just took a container of bread crumbs out of the cupboard. I plan to have chicken this evening. I try to eat only one meal a day when I am not fasting, preferably in the evening. Some of the ingredients listed are: mono and diglycerides, sodium and/or calium stearol lactylate, monocalcium phosphate, calcium sulfate, ammonium sulfate, calcium and propionate. Now after reading that, I am not hungry. I could go get a loaf of bread, toast a few slices and make my own bread crumbs; but who knows what they put in the bread?

Personally, I don't like to eat anything that has ingredients in it that I can't pronounce. I try to eat a lot of salads, fruits and nuts. We need to fast to cleanse

---

[14] Quote by Bill Winston.

our bodies from all the tonics and everything else that is unhealthy. Are you a coffee drinker? If you don't have a coffee in the morning, do you start to go off the wall a little until you get one? Maybe you're addicted to the caffeine, sugar and other things from a constant intake of them. Do you need to eat something sweet before you go to bed? Maybe its aspirins and something else your body is addicted to. This may be why when we fast our bodies hurt—because we are having withdrawals. We may experience some of the following symptoms: headaches, cramps, fever, dizziness, a tendency to vomit, severe sharp pains in the abdomen, weak knees, short breath, sleeplessness, nervousness, vexation, foul breath, watery nose. We may experience six of them over four days. Maybe one or two different ones at a time, never all of them at once; for the Lord will not give you more than you can handle.

Why does all this take place? The body is healing. Knowing this, it will be much easier resting, realizing the process is working. "When God finished His work of creation, He rested on the seventh day from all the work which He had done. Thus, God blessed the seventh day and hollowed it. As with God, rest is a reward to man for his work. It is a tonic for the tired, and a release from labor. Rest restores and relieves body, mind, and soul overwrought from various burdens."[15]

When you fast, it gives the digestive system, the nervous system and various other bodily systems rest. This is why, after about the fifth day, I am able to think and reason much better and clearer. Why? My body is

---

[15] Merrill C. Tenney, *The Zondervan Pictorial Encyclopedia of the Bible* (Grand Rapids: Zondervan 1975), 68.

not spending all that energy to digest food. Much more blood flows to the brain and not to the digestive system, because I ate three big greasy hot dogs loaded with mustard, relish, ketchup, onions, and celery salt. If you eat that, your breath will smell like you're fasting.

It's very important that during a fast you don't try to get up out of bed as fast as you normally would or stand up out of a chair too fast. You can become light headed if you attempt to get up quickly.

I have already mentioned that I always commit the fast to the Lord. The Lord will teach us all the things we need to learn about fasting as we step out in faith and fast. The more you meditate on Isaiah 58 the more you will learn about the heart of God regarding it. During or before a fast, I give the food that I would have eaten to the poor and needy. In God's Word, it states, "Is not this the kind of fasting I have chosen: to loose the chains of injustice and untie the cords of the yoke, to set the oppressed free and break every yoke? Is it not to share your food with the hungry and to provide the poor wanderer with shelter—when you see the naked, to clothe him, and not to turn away from your own flesh and blood" (Is. 58:6-7)? In the following verse, it talks about breakthrough. It says: "Then your light will break forth like the dawn, and your healing will quickly appear; then your righteousness will go before you, and the glory of the Lord will be your rear guard" (Is. 58:8).

Did you notice verse eight starts with the word "then." After verse six and seven, then the breakthrough. We have not looked at verse nine yet. It also starts with the word "then." Let's look at it. It reads: "Then you will call, and the Lord will answer; you will cry for help, and He will say: 'Here am I.' If you do away with the yoke of oppression, with the pointing finger and malicious talk, and if you spend yourselves in behalf of the hungry and satisfy the needs of the oppressed, then your light will rise in the darkness, and your night will become like the noonday" (Is. 58:9-10). The Lord states it again in verse ten regarding feeding the hungry. He says, "spend yourselves in behalf of the hungry." When we do things the Lord's way, then we get our breakthrough. If God's Word says it get ready. It will come to pass.

BREAKING A FAST

Breaking the fast is probably the most central part of the fast. After a five or six day fast with no food your stomach is like that of a newborn baby. Would you give a week old baby steak and eggs? The same way you would break in a new car motor, we have to break the fast slow. If I fast ten days no food, I would want it to take me ten days before I am eating the way I was before I started the fast. When breaking a fast the first day I would drink a glass of orange or grapefruit juice toward the end of the day. The second and third day I would have a couple of oranges or a big grapefruit at the end of the day. The fourth day I might have some nice hot vegetable soup and the next few days a light salad. You get the idea?

It takes hard work persevering through the trials and tribulations while fasting. If we break it in the wrong way we may jeopardize losing the positive benefits we receive spiritually, mentally and physically.

Lastly, I stay away from nuts and other foods that are hard to digest. Also, I stay away from milk when breaking a fast which may cause bloating. However, I enjoy small amounts of yogurt that seems to be good for me because it provides good bacteria and settles my stomach at times. I have to use wisdom around these Mexicans; tacos loaded with hot chili peppers are not the way to get the job done!

It's important to make your best effort to eat healthy when you're finished breaking the fast. Fasting will help tremendously to cleanse your body from a vast array of harmful things, some that are self-imposed and some that are not. It's important to be good stewards of God's temple. Remember the scripture that states: "Therefore, I urge you, brothers, in view of God's mercy, to offer your bodies as living sacrifices, holy and pleasing to God—this is your spiritual act of worship" (Ro. 12:1).

STEWARDSHIP

I am owner of nothing; however, I must not forget, I'm the steward of everything. This body is not mine; I was bought with a price. Those are concepts that I must incorporate into my life. Finances, relationships, children, ministries—everything a Christian has belongs to the Lord. The definition of the word stewardship is: "a person who manages another's property or financial affairs; one who administers anything as the agent of another."[16]

Please allow me to show you the scripture that confirms who the aforementioned owner of the world is. The verse is: "For by Him all things were created: things in heaven and on earth, visible and invisible, whether thrones or powers or rulers or authorities; all things were created by Him and for Him. He is before all things, and in Him all things hold together" (Col. 1:16). Another verse is: "Whom He appointed heir of all things, and through whom He made the universe" (Heb.1:2). That verse just told us "Jesus is heir of all things."

"Stewardship is the proper management of time, talent, and money for the glory of God."[17] Some Christians may want a new car but can't change the oil in the one they have now or throw away all the trash that's piled up in the back seat of the car. That is certainly not proper management. Some may not care about their car until someone asks if they can borrow

---

[16] Stewardship," www.dictionary.com

[17] Elmer L. Towns, *Fasting for Financial Breakthrough* (Ventura: Regal Books 2002), 44.

it, then they get very concerned. Some individuals may want a big house on the water but can't vacuum the rugs in the little apartment they have. That is certainly not proper management.

We are stewards of every penny that is entrusted to us by the Lord. The only way to manage these finances is through tithes and offerings. We have to be concerned with the little. If we manage that right, God will bring the increase.

After sixteen years at sea, I was taken off the ships and appointed as a union official for the National Maritime Union in the Port of Boston. A gentleman was in my office one day and he told me: "Take care of the pennies and the dollars will take care of themselves."

Proper management is vital in order to have life more abundantly. We must become skillful stewards of the resources entrusted to us by "the heir of all things." When God informed me to write on this subject, I started thinking of all the things of which I am a steward. We have to become experts in stewardship if we expect increase. God does not honor sloth and/or arrogance.

Some individuals may just lie around and expect God to deliver everything right to their doorstep. You may be waiting "until the cows come home, the moon turns green and the monkeys chew tobacco." I had to quote that. Rodney Howard Brown quoted that English saying years ago in a meeting.

God says: "Whoever sows sparingly will also reap sparingly, and whoever sows generously will also reap generously" (2 Cor. 9:6). He also says: "Be very careful, then, how you live—not as unwise but as wise, making the most of every opportunity, because the days are evil" (Eph. 5:15-16). There are only twenty-four hours in a day and we have to be good stewards of time. I want to share an experience with you.

I was going into my second year of Bible College and it was summer. I was volunteering my time in the office on campus answering the phone. I wanted to be sure I locked myself in a position where I could study over the summer to avoid idleness. I did that every summer and the Easter, Thanksgiving and Christmas breaks. Why, because I know how God works. I know that if you give, you receive. I didn't own any Commentaries, Topical Bibles, Bible Dictionaries, Bible Encyclopedias and a vast array of other Christian resource books that I really needed and wanted. I could have gotten a job and bought them but I wanted to give God my time. Besides, He knew exactly what I needed.

There was an evangelist coming in to town for revival services. I was able to save a few dollars and buy him a book on the gifts of the Holy Ghost. Well, right after I got that brand spanking new book into the man of God's hand, God moved. I was sitting at the desk answering the phone on campus. A gentleman called and stated that he was a professor who used to teach on campus. He said he had retired and was moving to Florida and he had a cellar full of books he was looking to give away. He asked me if I knew anyone that might be interested. I got his address and went seven blocks away to his house on my lunch break. There they were—all my Commentaries, Topical Bibles, Bible Dictionaries, Bible Encyclopedias and a vast array of other Christian resource books I needed. Praise God!

I sowed one book on the Holy Ghost to the man of God and I had to make trips with my car to bring in the blessings. Then the school blessed me for volunteering. The best part of the story is, I was able to "study to show myself approved unto God a worker who does not need to be ashamed, rightly dividing the word of truth" (2 Tim. 2:15).

Is there something you feel you need to sow? How are you managing God's time? Are you serving the Lord with the resources he has given you? I have a note on the inside of my car windshield. I read it often and I want to share it with you. It states: "Prepare me and I'll go. No, go and He'll prepare you." God has a standard for us to follow which will bless us with abundance when we submit to His ways. I remember receiving a call and someone informing me they had sent $15,000 to Zion Bible College for my tuition. It was summer time and I was on my way to New Jersey to see my favorite evangelist Ted Shuttlesworth. I'll never forget it. At that time, I was witnessing every day in a small park in Riverside, RI. The police showed up and said someone complained and asked me to stop preaching the Gospel. About one hundred individuals gave their hearts to the Lord over a two week period. Do you know, not everyone is happy when the Gospel is preached? I didn't care; it was starting to get up in the 80's. I had planned to move to the air conditioned Providence Place Mall anyway.

I was leaving for one week the following morning for New Jersey to hear Brother Ted. I am sure glad I went. He prophesied new bones into a man's back. It was totally incredible. While I was there, he preached on the following scripture: "Now he who supplies seed to the sower and bread for food will also supply and increase your store of seed and will enlarge the harvest of your righteousness" (2 Cor. 9:10).

He explained it so powerfully and it got in my Spirit. When I got back to my desk on the old

Stewardship

Barrington campus I sought the Lord. I said, "Lord, as you know, I have been tithing about one hundred and fifty dollars a month and sowing fifty dollars to missions in China. But Lord, I know in my Spirit I should increase it. I am going to start sowing one hundred and fifty rather than fifty into missions work."

I will never forget this as long as I live. It was ten minutes to nine and I had to wait ten minutes to call Brother Ted's office in West Virginia. I didn't know who or what to make the check payable to. At 9:05 I wrote that check out, licked the envelope and set it on my desk. Within twenty seconds my phone rang. It was a woman who explained to me that someone gave her my phone number and informed her, I was a painter. She said she lived three blocks from the campus and was looking for someone to paint her house for $1500. She said she had the paint and ladders in the garage if I was interested in doing the job. I informed her I was and that I would be right over.

I ended up painting that house in four days. I needed that $1500 to pay tithes on that $15,000 blessing. I went to the Salvation Army to preach, where I volunteered weekly, and I gave that testimony. A gentleman, who had been coming to those services to hear me preach for about a year, stated he would come and give me a hand. It's so important to be a good overseer of God's money and time.

"Satan hates God so much that he will use money to destroy God's work and His worker's. What did Satan use in his first attempt to destroy the New Testament Church? Money! Acts 5:1-11 tell of a rich husband and wife, leaders in the Church, who were blinded by greed. Ananias and Sapphira were envious of the public acclaim that Barnabus received for

Christians when he sold a piece of ground and gave all the proceeds to God. Ananias and Sapphira decided to sell their land as well. They wanted the same cheer from the crowd. However, after they sold their possession, the two of them decided to keep part of the money, while still seeking the public acclaim. Therefore, they let everyone think that they were giving the entire amount of the proceeds of their sale to God."[18]

It is imperative to do everything with the proper motives. God informs us to: "Do everything in love" (1 Cor. 16:14). Allow me to close out with two scriptures regarding stewardship. The Word of God states: "Each one should use whatever gift he has received to serve others, faithfully administering God's grace in its various forms" (1 Pet. 4:10); lastly, "Since an overseer is entrusted with God's work, he must be blameless—not overbearing, not quick-tempered, not given to drunkenness, not violent, not pursuing dishonest gain" (Titus 1:7).

---

[18] Ibid, 79.

AN ALTRUISTIC LIFESTYLE

I truly believe an altruistic lifestyle is one of the most, if not the most important key to having life and having it more abundantly. The Word of God makes it clear when it informs us: "He who sows bountifully will also reap bountifully" (2 Cor. 9:6). That scripture does not only refer to finances. That is a spiritual law given to us from God. It is similar to the law of gravity. The key is that they both work every time.

When I got out of a locked mental institution, God put individuals in my life to get me to pray to Him and seek His face. These individuals informed me they needed me to get sobered up and stay straight so I could help them carry coffins of those who couldn't and/or wouldn't. They said it was important for me to live life on an altruistic plane—that I had to give away everything that I received from God.

When I got to Bible College I bought a big box of 9 by 12 yellow envelopes and every time I wrote a paper for a professor I would also mail them to everyone I knew. I also e-mailed them to many libraries where I visited often, and asked individuals that worked in the reference department to proofread them for me. Even though they had already been proofread, I just wanted to give away what God gave me. Besides, having them proofread them several times is better than just once. I guess you could call me an email evangelist. Praise God!

I remember for years going back to the locked mental institutions every week telling people about the love of Jesus and seeing people filled with the Holy Ghost after they received the Lord. I recall one man in particular. He visited the Salvation Army in

An Altruistic Lifestyle

Providence, RI. He stated he was on the third floor in his apartment and he wanted to jump out the window and commit suicide. He received Jesus and then I prayed with him for the baptism of the Holy Spirit. He got so infused with power from on High he left the building and went right to the yellow line in the middle of the road. He kept jumping up and down waving his arms yelling "I'm free, I'm free." As far as my eye could see he went right up the middle of the road yelling "I'm free in Jesus." That sounds a whole lot better than jumping out a third floor window. I recall someone once calling me a "Holy Roller." I told him: "Praise God! I'm grateful I'm rolling in the right direction."

I used to be a lexicographer. The definition of a lexicographer is: "a writer, editor, or compiler of a dictionary."[19] I wrote dictionaries for books to be used as study guides to help individuals with various additions. I wrote four different dictionaries in total. So you must know I like and respect words. Please permit me to define the word altruistic for you. It is defined as: "unselfishly concerned for or devoted to the welfare of others"[20]

I recall the saddest time while at sea when I attempted to help someone and failed. I was a boatswain in the Merchant Marines for sixteen years and sailed to about forty-five countries on huge cargo vessels. On one particular trip, we had the starboard anchor in the water while off the coast of Aruba and launch service was provided to take crewmembers ashore. It was an 800 foot oil taker and she was empty leaving the main deck, approximately sixty feet above

---

[19] Lexicographer," www.dictionary.com

[20] Altruistic," www.dictionary.com

the water's edge. One of the crewmembers had to go ashore to go to the doctor. He was a big man over 350 pounds. He fell off the ladder in the water. I jumped in and tried to get a line around him lowered down from a crewmember on deck, because the man couldn't swim. However, I couldn't tell the swells where so huge, prior to jumping in, because the view from sixty feet above was distorted. He did drown, and before he did, he kept trying to grab me. When I finally got on the ladder totally exhausted, I looked up and saw a bunch of heads looking over the rail. Only the third mate and myself made an attempt to help the man.

The church is on the deck where it's safe and comfortable. The heathens are in the water and will drown if we don't let God use us to pull them out. Our Christian walk with Christ Jesus must be on an altruistic plane. We may have to plunge into many dangerous and risky spots; however, if we do it with love being the motive, the Lord will always keep our heads above water, so we can preach His gospel.

Do you recall the discussion regarding the discipline of submission? We talked about what Jesus the king of Glory had to say which is as follows: "If anyone would come after Me, he must deny himself and take up his cross and follow Me. For whoever wants to save his life will lose it, but whoever loses his life for Me and for the gospel will save it" (Mk. 8:34-35). Jesus made it quite clear that self-denial is the only way to love ourselves.

Well, I thought I was done here, however, the Lord wants to talk to you some more on this subject. Let me explain to you how I know. Years ago when I was right in the middle of what I have been writing to you about in this chapter, God sent me a young man who needed some help. We became friends. He got married and had children and moved out in the country. It was back in 2001 when I met him. While I was writing this today, I often thought about this man and his wife. We have not been in close contact for many years. Well ten minutes ago I checked my e-mail and there was a message from him through facebook. I don't mess with facebook; however, the Lord wants me to have my contact information on there should someone try to reach me as this particular friend just did.

The message was this. "I need help" along with his phone number. We talked for thirty minutes and he rededicated his life back to the Lord. He informed me he would like to attend a Christian church in the area where he lives. I emailed him church information for that area. The point I have to make is that when you have Jesus, when you're walking in the Spirit of Almighty God, when you rightly divide the Word of truth, people know where to go when they need help. They know Gene will be there for them. *Let me contact Gene. I know Gene will drop everything he's doing and drive out and talk with me over a coffee.* And though my friend never knew that I'm now living on the border of Mexico, I just poured some good old fashioned love on him as best I could.

It is vital to always remember, love fails only when we fail to love. Can I ask you a question? Are you willing to put the time in to assist others? Can people put their trust in you that you will be there for them whenever they need your help? Are you willing to love on them and put their needs first? Possibly, years down the road when they need help and feel all alone, they will remember your altruistic lifestyle, and say to themselves, *I had better pick up the phone.*

GOD LOVES ORDER

First Corinthians is one of my favorite books in the Bible. I will reveal in this writing how God overshadowed the church at Corinth with divine insight and spiritual enrichment through His servant, the apostle Paul. The major concerns Paul had regarding the church were: "Divisions, disorder, and difficulties in the church."[21]

"Corinth was the largest city in first-century Greece, serving as capital of the Roman province of Achaia. It prospered due to its location on a narrow (about 3.5 miles wide) neck of land, or isthmus, between seas to the east and west. Most shipping heading to or from Rome passed through Corinth. Cargo was unloaded on one side of the isthmus, transported across, and reloaded onto another boat on the other side. Small boats with intact cargo may have been skidded across on a path constructed for that purpose. Corinth was thus an important center of commercial and social interchange.

Corinth was famous not only for its bustling trade and wealth but also its immorality. Greco-Roman sexual practices, never lofty by biblical standards, descended to remarkable lows in the form of extensive and lucrative prostitution. This activity was sometimes part of pagan worship and may help explain the sexual excesses among the Corinthian believers: Paul mentions that prior to their conversion to Christ, some of the Corinthians had been "sexually immoral,"

---

[21] George Knight and James Edwards, *Compact Bible Handbook* (Nashville: Thomas Nelson, Inc., 2004), 256.

"idolaters," "adulterers," "male prostitutes," and "homosexual offenders" (See 1 Cor. 6:9, 11). Through Christ, however, there was liberation from such dehumanizing practices."[22]

We can draw conclusions on the aforementioned; God's people were in serious need of spiritual guidance and correction. Therefore, Paul writes with instruction for the church. He states: "Brothers, stop thinking like children. In regard to evil be infants, but in your thinking be adults" (1Cor, 14:20). The believers in Corinth were immature and there was disorder and difficulties. This gave power to the false teacher, which in turn led to confusion in the people. Much divine insight was needed to allow spiritual expansion among God's people.

"Conviction of sin comes only by the Holy Spirit. But only rarely does He bypass human instrumentality in speaking to the hearts of sinful people. The means He uses is the message of the gospel delivered by faithful witnesses, for whom Paul stresses a need in Romans 10:9-17. The book of Acts chronicles the message of the Early Church. It consisted basically of the message of Jesus Christ as the Savior and the need to believe in Him on the basis of His death and resurrection, lest the judgment of God come upon the hearers if they reject Him. The result of this kind of Spirit-inspired witnessing was that people were 'cut to the heart' and asked, 'What shall we do?' (Acts 2:37). The Holy Spirit alone can convict and convince people of their need for salvation. The believers' responsibility is to declare and share the message of salvation, and to

---

[22] Walter A. Elwell and Robert W. Yarbrough, *Encountering the New Testament* (Grand Rapids: Baker Publishing Group, 1998), 288.

leave the results in the Lord's hands as He speaks to hearts by His Spirit."[23]

Convict, Convince, Conviction

The Holman Bible Dictionary defines conviction as: "A sense of guilt and shame leading to repentance. The words 'convict' and 'conviction' do not appear in the King James Version. The word 'convince' (KJV) comes closest to expressing the meaning of 'conviction.' The Hebrew word *yakah* expresses the idea of conviction. It means 'to argue with,' 'to prove,' 'to correct.' God may be the subject and persons the object (Job 22:4) or a person may be the subject who convicts another person (Ezekiel 3:26). The Greek term meaning 'convict' is *elegxo*. It means 'to convict' 'to refute,' 'to confute,' usually with the suggestion of shame of the person convicted."[24]

Secrets of the Heart

Paul had this to say: "...and the secrets of his heart will be laid bare. So he will fall down and worship God, exclaiming, 'God is really among you'" (1 Cor. 14:25). Adam Clark's input regarding this verse is: "As these, who were the prophets or teachers, had often the discernment of spirits, they were able in certain cases, and probably very frequently, to tell a

---

[23] Anthony D. Palma, *The Holy Spirit: A Pentecostal Perspective* (Springfield: Gospel Publishing House, 1973), 68.

[24] Studylight.org, *The Holman Bible Dictionary*, , accessed 7 April 2007; available from http://www. studylight.org/dic/hbd/view.cgi?number=T1399; Internet.

man the secrets of his own heart; and, where this was not directly the case, God often led His ministers to speak those things that were suitable to the case before them, though they themselves had no particular design. The sinner, therefore, convinced that God alone could uncover the secrets of his heart, would be often obliged to fall down on his face, abashed and confounded, and acknowledge that God was truly among them. This seems to be the plain meaning of the passages before us."[25] I really love what *The Commentary Critical and Explanatory on the Whole Bible* adds regarding this verse. They expand by stating: "He sees his own inner character opened out by the sword of the Spirit (Heb. 4:12; Jas. 1:23), the Word of God, in the hand of him who prophesieth. Compare the same effect produced on Nebuchadnezzar (Da. 2:30 and end of Da. 2:47)."

Like A Flash

"No argument is stronger for the truth of religion than its manifestation of men to themselves in their true character. Hence hearers even now often think the preacher must have aimed his sermon particularly at them."[26] An influential Swiss Protestant Reformed scholar of his day writes: "Every utterance of a prophet is like a flash, lighting up the heart of the

---

[25] Studylight.com, *The Adam Clarke Commentary*, accessed 7 April 2007; available from http://www.studylight.org/com/acc/view.cgi?book=1co&chapter=0 14; Internet.

[26] Studylight.org, *Commentary Critical and Explanatory on the Whole Bible*, accessed 7 April 2007; available from http://www.studylight.org/com/jfb/ view.cgi?book=1co&chapter=014; Internet.

hearer and discovering to him in a general way his guilt and defilement."[27]

Exegetical Assessments are Deep-seated

It is so important to properly use the spirituals gifts entrusted to us by our Heavenly Father. The Holy Spirit guides us into all truth, some of us faster than others. When I get filled, I am compelled to preach; because it has to come out in order to bless others.

Also, it has allowed growth and maturity so I can bear fruit for King Jesus. Maturity must be our main focus. We must mature; however, our Father in heaven is a God of order. When we receive Godly guidance and correction, we must incorporate them into our Christian walk with Christ. These will eliminate division, disorder and difficulties in our Christian life, relationships, character and our church.

---

[27] Frederic L. Godet, *Commentary on First Corinthians* (Grand Rapids: Kregel Publications, 1977), 724.

BECOME LIKE LITTLE CHILDREN

Do you want to spend eternity in heaven with King Jesus? This is what He says must happen in order to do so. Jesus states, "I tell you the truth, unless you change and become like little children, you will never enter the kingdom of heaven" (Mt. 18:3). The reason this book is geared toward spiritual growth is so you can become like little children. It can only be accomplished through faith, meditating on the Word and spiritual disciplines.

We must become Christ-like and continue to mature. The writer of the book of Hebrews says it like this: "Therefore let us leave the elementary teachings about Christ and go on to maturity, not laying again the foundation of repentance from acts that lead to death" (Heb. 6:1).

We cannot allow mental and/or emotional attachments to impinge upon spiritual development. Fretting and being anxious regarding the cares of this world are a booby trap from the kingdom of darkness. Doctor Luke informs us in the book of Luke: "The seed which fell among the thorns, these are the ones who have heard, and as they go on their way they are choked with worries and riches and pleasures of this life, and bring no fruit to maturity" (Lk. 8:14).

A Christian friend and his son would stop by the house and visit from time to time. I would ask his son to lay hands on me. He would put his hand on my chest and say: "Fill him up Jesus. Give him more Lord. Holy Spirit let his cup run over. Fill him up Jesus. Give him more Lord." He would do that for two to three minutes and God's love would take a powerful hold of me. God will use little children mightily if they are given the opportunity. Instead of the pastors and the deacons praying for the children, maybe the children should be praying for the pastors and deacons. Do you know what the very last verse in the Old Testament is? Let me give it to you: "He will restore the hearts of the fathers to their children and the hearts of the children to their fathers, so that I will not come and smite the land with a curse." (Mal. 4:6 NASB).

In the book I wrote titled *Pearls of Wisdom and Gems of Knowledge Regarding Christianity,* I wrote about a very powerful man of God named Count Zinzendorf. I was very glad when I found that a movie had been made on this incredible saint. "It is published by Christianity Today Inc. and bears the title *First Fruits.*"[28]

I watched this wonderful movie and in it there were scenes of congregations back in the 1700's. I notice the children were all seated in the first five rows with the adults sitting behind them. I write all this to help you draw conclusions. Do you think it's possible that children can help us more than we give them credit for? Do you think you need to draw closer to your own children and participate in more ministries together? Do you feel they can assist you to become more like a little child so you can spend eternity in heaven with King Jesus?

I would like to close out this chapter with an experience I had. The Mexican people are very relational. I was invited to a Christian church in Victoria, Mexico, by my friend, so I went. The size of the congregation was about 400 and it was Father's

---

[28] Christian History Institute. www.chi.gospelcom.net

Become Like Little Children

Day. At the end of the service, the big back doors of the sanctuary swung open and hundreds of children ran to their fathers to embrace them. As soon as those doors swung open, I felt the powerful love of God sweep through that congregation. I have never experienced anything like it before. That incident leaves me to wonder… Is the love of God stronger in the children's lives or the adults?

OUR RESPONSE TO AUTHORITY

I asked the Holy Spirit to use these fingers of clay as an instrument to type on this subject matter with clarity and oratorical finesse that it would be pleasing in the sight of the Almighty God who sits on His throne. First and foremost, I must make this statement: "All sins release the power of death, but the sin of rebellion releases it the most."[29]

Are you aware that everywhere you go God has authority set in place? Please allow me to illustrate. God gives authority to the owner of a store. The owner gives authority to the manager. The manager gives authority to the individual at the cash register. And then you go in the store and argue with the person at the register. Are you not arguing with God's authority?

It reminds me when I went into a store to use the copy machine years ago. As I was somewhat confused as to how it worked, the gentleman at the register came over and started screaming at me. I said to him, "Thank you for that information. Is there anything else you can tell me that will help me to be a better customer in the future?" I disarmed him with love.

We know Moses was God's servant and was given authority by God. Let's take a look in the fourth book in the Bible called Numbers. It reads: "The next day the whole Israelite community grumbled against Moses and Aaron. 'You have killed the Lord's people,' they said. But when the assembly gathered in

---

[29] Watchman Nee, *Spiritual Authority* (New York: Christian Fellowship Publishers, Inc. 1972), 71.

opposition to Moses and Aaron and turned toward the Tent of Meeting, suddenly the cloud covered it and the glory of the Lord appeared. Then Moses and Aaron went to the front of the Tent of Meeting, and the Lord said to Moses, 'Get away from this assembly so I can put an end to them at once.' And they fell facedown. Then Moses said to Aaron, 'Take your censer and put incense in it, along with fire from the altar, and hurry to the assembly to make atonement for them. Wrath has come out from the Lord; the plague has started.' So Aaron did as Moses said, and ran into the midst of the assembly. The plague had already started among the people, but Aaron offered the incense and made atonement for them. He stood between the living and the dead, and the plague stopped. But 14,700 people died from the plague, in addition to those who had died because of Korah. Then Aaron returned to Moses at the entrance to the Tent of Meeting, for the plague had stopped" (Nu. 16:41-50).

We can see what happens when individuals rebel against the authority that God sets in place. Some individuals may not understand the wrath of God. Wrath is judgment: it is what God does, not what He is. Knowing God's divine attributes helps us to understand God's wrath. God is love. God is also holy. Wrath comes because of God's holiness. Also, God is just. The Bible says: "God is just. He will pay back trouble to those who trouble you" (2 Th. 1:6). We know for sure that God cannot lie.

God's justice overrides man's righteousness. We are serving a holy God. The scriptures say: "As obedient children, do not conform to the evil desires you had when you lived in ignorance. But just as He who called you is holy, so be holy in all you do; for it is written: 'Be holy, because I am holy'" (1 Pet. 1:14-16).

Our Response to Authority

Allow me to give you another illustration. God gives authority to the senior pastor. The senior pastor gives authority to the youth pastor. The youth are having an event and the youth pastor gives authority to the individuals that are serving out in the parking lot. You drive in the parking lot and you argue with the attendant. My question to you is, who are you arguing with?

Let's take a look at the life of King David. He was a mighty warrior. David was a man of faith who knew how to pray and fast. He knew how to worship the Lord. He understood spiritual authority. David knew how to win battles against the enemies. David had wisdom and knew how and when to act as though he was insane. David knew how to dance in the Holy Ghost. By reading the Psalms that David wrote, we know David had a heart after God. David said: "Praise be to the Lord my Rock, who trains my hands for war, my fingers for battle" (Ps. 144:1). Do you know how God trained David for battle? God had King Saul chase David around for fifteen years trying to kill him. David had to submit to God's authority.

There is authority set in place even for angels, who are spirit beings. The Bible informs us: "Though you already know all this, I want to remind you that the Lord delivered His people out of Egypt, but later destroyed those who did not believe. And the angels who did not keep their positions of authority but abandoned their own home—these He has kept in darkness, bound with everlasting chains for judgment on the great Day. In a similar way, Sodom and Gomorrah and the surrounding towns gave themselves up to sexual immorality and perversion. They serve as an example of those who suffer the punishment of eternal fire. In the very same way, these dreamers pollute their own bodies, reject authority and slander celestial beings. But even the archangel Michael when he was disputing with the devil about the body of Moses, did not dare to bring a slanderous accusation against him, but said, 'The Lord rebuke you'" (Jude 1: 5-9)!

Rules of Submission for Christian Households

"Wives submit to your husbands, as is fitting in the Lord. Husbands love your wives and do not be harsh with them. Children, obey your parents in everything, for this pleases the Lord. Fathers, do not embitter your children, or they will become discouraged. Slaves obey your earthly masters in everything; and do it, not only when their eye is on you and to win their favor, but with sincerity of heart and reverence for the Lord. Whatever you do, work at it with all your heart, as working for the Lord, not for men, since you know that you will receive an inheritance from the Lord as a reward. It is the Lord Christ you are serving. Anyone who does wrong will be repaid for his wrong and there is no favoritism" (Col. 3:18-25).

Well, we certainly need to know the truth. It is the only thing that will set us free. The Lord informs us in His Word: "For rebellion is as the sin of witchcraft, and stubbornness is as iniquity and idolatry" (1 Sam. 15:23 NKJV). This is very strong language and we certainly cannot take it lightly.

I have a question for you. Are you thinking, what if the person in authority is wrong? Well that's a good question and I want to give you an answer. "The answer is, if God dares to entrust His authority to men, and then we can dare to obey. Whether the one in authority is right or wrong does not concern us, since he has to be responsible directly to God. The obedient needs only to obey; the Lord will not hold us responsible for any mistaken obedience, rather will He hold the delegated authority responsible for his erroneous act. Insubordination, however, is rebellion, and for this the one under authority must answer to God."[30]

Youth, I have a question for you. Will you be submitting to your teachers when they tell you something you do not want to hear? How about when your parents ask you to clean your room? Adults, I have a question for you. Will you be submitting to your boss and the people that God has put over you when they tell you something you do not want to hear? I truly hope this material has blessed you and has given you fresh insight, which will help you make wise decisions in the future regarding authority and submission. Well, I am not sure who the author was, however, years ago I read: "Your response to authority determines your life's progress."

---

[30] Ibid, 71.

ENTER HIS REST

As I mentioned earlier, there is only one step; that is to step in. "We are seated in heavenly places in Christ" (Eph. 2:6). By faith just step in. "God has blessed us in the heavenly realms with every spiritual blessing in Christ" (Eph.1:3). By faith just step in. "His divine power has given us everything we need for life and godliness" (1 Pt. 1:3). By faith just step in. "Come boldly unto the throne of grace, that we may obtain mercy, and find grace to help in time of need" (Heb. 4:16). By faith just step in. "Be still, and know that I am God" (Ps. 46:10). By faith just step in. "Make every effort to enter that rest" (Heb. 4:11).

What else is there? I tried everything else. I traveled to about forty-five countries and have seen the world. I thought relationships with different women of unusual nationalities would get the job done, but that failed. I gambled high stakes in Vegas, Atlantic City, Porto Rico and the Caribbean. I fished giant tuna, shark, marlin and sailfish. I had Jaguars, Cadillacs and Lincolns. I owned all kinds of fishing boats. I had a garage full of Harley Davidson's. I have been on many huge shopping sprees. I did heroin, coke and every drug under the sun. All that nonsense and running around looking for love, peace, joy and contentment brought me emptiness in the end. All I really had to do was to step in with the Lord.

I wonder how many Christians are still missing it by running all around with busyness and yet they are still missing it. You might be saying, "Oh you're being hard brother Gene." No, I'm not being hard... I'm merely preaching the Gospel. Everything is finished you have need of whether it's something spiritual and/or material. Just receive it by faith right now. Faith is always right now. When you're in time you're out of faith. The Bible says, "Faith is" meaning present tense. Faith is always right now. Rest in faith and His love right now.

Go with me over to the book of Matthew chapter eleven. My Bible is in red letters. That means Jesus Himself said, "Come to me, all you who are weary and burdened, and I will give you rest" (Mt. 11:28). Jesus wants to give me rest? Can I give you the definition in the Greek for the word "rest" in that verse? It is: "to keep quiet, of calm and patient expectation."

Christians need to continually rest in God's love rather than run all around with busyness. Let me give you scriptures to confirm what I am saying. The Bible says: "I have given you authority to trample on snakes and scorpions and to overcome all the power of the enemy; nothing will harm you" (Lk. 10:19). We have been given "all authority." First Timothy informs me how people in authority must live. It says: "all those in authority, that we may live peaceful and quiet lives in all godliness and holiness" (1 Tim. 2:2).

We must rest in Him. Our salvation is in Him. Our salvation is in the rest. Here's a scripture that confirms it: "This is what the Sovereign Lord, the Holy One of Israel, says: 'In repentance and rest is your salvation, in quietness and trust is your strength, but you would have none of it'" (Is. 30:15). There it is!

There is no short cut. Everything is in God's love. We must rest in faith and God's love. I already informed you I tried all the other avenues. I tried black shoelaces, brown shoelaces and gray shoe laces. There is nothing else other than to become experts with the heavy equipment God has given us.

Enter His Rest

May I share an experience with you? In 2010, the Lord gave me fresh vision for a new season. The Lord released me from school after five years. He informed me to go into Victoria, Mexico for ministry. The day before I started writing this book, I had my feet up on the desk and was looking out the window. They have been turning the road in front of the house from two lanes to four lanes. They have been out there for three months. I was watching all the different types of heavy equipment operate and watched them move all around. This is when the Lord said to me: "Gene do you realize all the things I had to move around so that you are where you are in Me, ready to go down this new road I have for you? Your Christian education, your calling, your gifting and everything else I have done in you? I have done a mighty work in you so now just rest in Me and watch what I do through you. Just rest in Me and watch what I do through you. Just rest in Me. Just rest in Me."

About an hour later while resting in Him, a gigantic backhoe with a huge shovel showed up. The equipment operator took the shovel and was picking it up and dropping it. Picking it up and dropping it. The whole house started shaking, especially the windows. The Lord said to me: "I am going to use you to shake the nations. Have faith and just rest in Me and watch what I do through you. Have faith and just rest in Me and watch what I do through you. Have faith and just rest in Me. Just rest in Me."

DAILY FAITH CONFESSIONS

(These are not direct quotations from the Bible but
are paraphrased confessions based on scripture.)
SAY THEM OUT LOUD.

I am God's child (Jn. 1:12). I am royalty (1 Pet. 2:9). I
am hidden with Christ in God (Col. 3:3). I am united
with the Lord (1 Cor. 6:17). I am a friend of Christ
(Jn. 15:15). I am raised up with Him, and seated with
Him in heavenly places in Christ Jesus (Eph. 2:6). I
was bought with a price (1 Cor. 6:19-20). I am
blessed when I come in, and blessed shall I be when
I go out (Deut. 28:6). I am a personal witness of
Christ (Acts 1:8). I am a saint who prays in the Holy
Spirit to keep myself in the love of God (Jude 1:20-
21). I draw near with confidence to the throne of
grace (Heb. 4:16). I have been adopted by the Father
(Eph. 1:5). I am the salt and light of the earth (Mt.
5:13). I am the head and not the tail, and I am above,
and not underneath. I am the lender and not the
borrower (Deut. 28:13). I have authority to trample
serpents and scorpions and over all the power of the
enemy (Lk. 10:19). I am a member of the body of
Christ (1 Cor. 12:27). God blessed me to be fruitful,
and multiply, and replenish the earth, and subdue it:
and have dominion (Gen. 1:28). I cannot be
separated from God's love (Ro. 8:39). The good work
God has begun in me will be perfected (Phil. 1:5). I
can do all things through Christ who strengthens me
(Phil. 4:13). No weapon that is formed against me
will prosper (Is. 54:17). So then faith cometh by
hearing, and hearing by the word of God (Ro. 10:17
KJV). Faith is my currency to operate in the kingdom

of God (Ro. 14:23). I am God's workmanship created in Christ Jesus for good works, which God prepared beforehand (Eph. 2:10). I have been appointed to bear fruit, and that my fruit would remain (Jn. 15:16). I am being wise when I am winning souls for King Jesus (Pr. 11:30). My body is the temple of the Holy Spirit (1 Cor. 6:19). I have access to God through the Holy Spirit (Eph. 2:18). I have been justified (Ro. 5:1). Therefore there is now no condemnation for those who are in Christ Jesus (Ro. 8:1). Greater is He who is in me than he who is in the world (1 Jn. 4:4). I will do greater works than Jesus because He went to the Father (Jn. 14:12). As God was with Moses, He will be with me; God will not fail me or forsake me (Jos. 1:5). I see myself the way God see me. God sees me as a king (Gen, 17:6, Rev. 1:6) God sees me as royalty (1 Pet. 2:9). God sees me as the righteousness of God in Christ, bold as a lion (Ro. 3:22, Pr. 28:1). God sees me without spot or wrinkle because of the blood of Jesus (1 Pet. 1:19). I am having faith for big things because God owns everything and I'm His son (Ps. 24:1). No man will be able to stand before me all the days of my life (Jos. 1:5). My Father is glorified by this that I bear much fruit, and proves I'm a disciple (see Jn. 15:8). I think big and confess big things because God is big (Ps. 24:1). I will respect God for the big God that He is and my mouth will create whatever I want (Lk. 6:45). I no longer think of millions, my renewed mind thinks of billions because the wealth of the wicked is laid up for the righteous (Pr. 13:22). The sinner's job is to gather and collect for the one who is good in God's sight (Ecc. 2:26). Redemption is not complete without prosperity. Jesus hung on the cross so I can have the whole package, not just salvation (2 Cor. 8:9). I don't have to qualify, Jesus has qualified me. Jesus reversed the curse. The devil is a liar, and Jesus is the Messiah. Jesus is made unto me wisdom, righteousness, sanctification, and redemption (1 Cor. 1:30). I submit to God, I resist the devil and he flees from me (Jas. 4:7). For God has not given me the spirit of fear; but of power, and of love, and of a sound mind (2 Tim. 1:7). The Holy Spirit will teach me all things (Jn. 14:26). The Holy Spirit will guide me into all truth (Jn.16:13). The Holy Spirit abides in me, and I don't need anyone to teach me, but the anointing teaches me all things (1 Jn. 2:27). I quench fiery darts from the wicked one with the shield of faith (Eph. 6:16). I stand firm against the schemes of the devil (Eph. 6:11). I already have the victory and Satan cannot back me up. I advance and hold. Advance and hold to victory after victory (2 Cor. 2:14). I walk in love and live by faith (Gal. 5:6). I have been redeemed from the curse of the law, poverty, sickness, and spiritual death (Gal. 3:13; Deut. 28). I bear much fruit. I'm God's workmanship created beforehand for good works (Eph. 2:10). God's favor is on my life (Ps. 3:8). God blesses me and His favor surrounds me as with a shield (Ps. 5:12). The kingdom of God is within me (Lk. 17:21). I have a production plant inside of me that bears fruit to change the world (Gen. 1:28). God gives me power to get wealth to establish His covenant on earth (Deut. 8:18). I am blessed to be a blessing (Gen. 12:2). I have Satan on the run and will make a mockery of him (Jas. 4:7). No man will be able to stand before me all the days of my life (Jos. 1:5). God's angels keep me in all my ways (Ps. 91:11).

PRAYER FOR SALVATION

Say the following prayer out loud.

Heavenly Father, I am a sinner and I need a Savior. I confess Jesus Christ as the Lord of my life. I repent of all my sins. Father, I truly believe you raised Jesus from the dead. I pray this prayer in Jesus' name. Father, I am your child because Jesus is my Lord. I want to receive the fullness of the Holy Spirit. Holy Spirit come into me and fill me so I can be a mighty witness for King Jesus. I pray this prayer in Jesus' name. Amen.

PRAYER FOR BAPTISM OF THE HOLY SPIRIT

Say the following prayer out loud.

Father, I am your child because Jesus is my Lord. Jesus said, "How much more shall your heavenly Father give the Holy Spirit to those who ask Him." I ask you now in the name of Jesus to fill me with the Holy Spirit. Thank you, Father, I received the baptism of the Holy Spirit by faith. I yield my vocal organs and expect to speak in tongues as the Holy Spirit gives me utterance in Jesus name. Father, I plan to pray in the Holy Spirit building myself up on my most holy faith, and keep myself in the love of God, as mentioned in Jude 20 and 21. In Jesus name I decree it. Amen.

ABOUT THE AUTHOR

Eugene Carvalho is an administrator, Christian author of one hundred twenty books, and the founder of Receiving by Faith. God uses him in the offices of pastor, evangelist and prophet. He holds a bachelor's degree in biblical studies and a double minor in pastoral ministry and world missions. He also holds a master's degree in practical theology. Eugene prayed for a translator and God sent his wife Mercedes who has a six-year degree in Spanish from a university in Tampico, Mexico. They have participated in evangelism in the streets of Mexico for many years. They have also traveled to churches all over the United States and the nation of Mexico winning souls and preaching the gospel of the kingdom. Their website for their ministry is: www.receivingbyfaith.org.

BOOKS BY EUGENE IN ENGLISH

For a complete list of other books by Eugene visit receivingbyfaith.org or amazon.com.

Receiving by Faith
Faith for Every Day: 365 Daily Devotions
Faith Cometh by Hearing, and Hearing by the Word of God
Faith, Hope, and Love
Walk in Love and Live by Faith
Topical Christian Handbook and Scripture Guide
The Gospel Is the Power of God unto Salvation
Seed Time and Harvest Time
Your New Identity in Christ
The Cross and the Blood
The Holy Spirit
The Attributes of God
The Favor of God
The Glory of God
The Grace of God
The Power of God
The Promises of God
The Throne of God
The Holy Spirit Will Guide You into All Truth
The New Testament Church: A Survey from the Book of Ephesians
Vengeance and Recompense
God's Angel's
Prayer and Fasting
God's Mighty Prophets
A Survey of Jesus Through the Epistles

You Have Authority and Power: Take Back What
the Devil Stole
Be Strong and Courageous
Prayer and Praise: The Big Artillery
Apostles and Prophets: The Foundation of the
Church
Covenant: A Concise Survey
Sow Then Reap a Harvest
God Has Not Given Us a Spirit of Timidity, But of
Power, Love, and Discipline
Blessed and Highly Favored
Grace and Peace Be Multiplied Unto You
Your Word Is a Lamp to Me Feet
John: A Key Word Study Made Simple
For Momentary, Light Affliction Is Producing For
Us an Eternal Weight of Glory
Prayer Is Powerful: What the Bible Has to Say
My People Are Destroyed By Lack of Knowledge
God Deserves Pure Worship
The Mouth of the Righteous is a Fountain of Life
The Lord Requires Integrity: The Major Element of
Leadership
Weeping May Last for the Night, But a Shout of
Joy Comes in the Morning
A Topical Look at the Book of Deuteronomy
A Topical Look at the Book of Psalms
A Topical Look at the Book of Proverbs
A Topical Look at the Book of Isaiah
A Topical Look at the Book of John
A Topical Look at the Book of Hebrews
A Topical Look at the Book of Revelation

BOOKS BY EUGENE IN SPANSIH

Las Promesas de Dios
Los Salmos de David
Lo Sobrenatural: Lo que la Bíblia Tiene que Decir
Una Mirada Topica Del Libro De Los Salmos
Dios es Amor: Lo que la Biblia Tiene que Decir
La Adquisición de la Sabiduría es Vital: Lo que la
Biblia Tiene que Decir

NOTES

NOTES

NOTES

<u>NOTES</u>